The Class

by Beatrice Reynolds

PEARSON

Scott
Foresman

Editorial Offices: Glenview, Illinois • Parsippany, New Jersey • New York, New York
Sales Offices: Needham, Massachusetts • Duluth, Georgia • Glenview, Illinois
Coppell, Texas • Ontario, California • Mesa, Arizona

Every effort has been made to secure permission and provide appropriate credit for photographic material. The publisher deeply regrets any omission and pledges to correct errors called to its attention in subsequent editions.

Unless otherwise acknowledged, all photographs are the property of Scott Foresman, a division of Pearson Education.

Photo locators denoted as follows: Top (T), Center (C), Bottom (B), Left (L), Right (R), Background (Bkgd)

Opener: Rubberball Productions; 3 Rubberball Productions; 4 ©DK Images; 5 ©DK Images; 6 (BR) © Comstock Inc., (BL) ©DK Images; 7 Getty Images; 8 (T) Rubberball Productions, (B) Corbis

ISBN: 0-328-13164-4

1 2 3 4 5 6 7 8 9 10 V0G1 14 13 12 11 10 09 08 07 06 05

Here is a class. What things could they do? What do you do in your class?

The class can make a farm. Look at the horse. Look at the duck. Look at the old pig. What do you make in your class?

4

The class can go to the park. The kids play. They have fun. Where do you go with your class?

The class has a pet. Blake takes care of the class pet and its cage. That is his job. What job can you do in your class?

Kids help in the class. Drake can put paper on the desk. Sage can set the pens in place. How can you be a helper in your class?

It is time for the class to go. The kids get on the bus. Do you get on a bus too?